Johannes Brahms

COMPLETE CONCERTI

in Full Score

From the Breitkopf & Härtel Complete Works Edition

Edited by Hans Gál

Dover Publications, Inc.
New York

Published in Canada by General Publishing Company, Ltd., 30 Lesmill Road, Don Mills, Toronto, Ontario.
Published in the United Kingdom by Constable and Company, Ltd., 10 Orange Street, London WC2H 7EG.

This Dover edition, first published in 1981, is an unabridged republication of Volume 6 *(Konzerte für Klavier und Orchester)* and Volume 5 *(Konzerte für Streichinstrumente und Orchester)* of *Johannes Brahms; Sämtliche Werke; Ausgabe der Gesellschaft der Musikfreunde in Wien*, originally published by Breitkopf & Härtel, Leipzig, n.d. (Editor's Commentary to Vol. 5 dated Summer 1926; to Vol. 6, Spring 1927). The Editor's Commentary was translated by Stanley Appelbaum specially for the present edition.

International Standard Book Number: 0-486-24170-X
Library of Congress Catalog Card Number: 81-66302

Manufactured in the United States of America
Dover Publications, Inc.
180 Varick Street
New York, N.Y. 10014

CONTENTS

EDITOR'S COMMENTARY

PIANO CONCERTO NO. 1 IN D MINOR, OP. 15

SOURCE TEXTS:

1. The score edition of the Verlag Rieter-Biedermann (now C. F. Peters in Leipzig).
2. Brahms's personal working copy of the score, in the possession of the Gesellschaft der Musikfreunde in Vienna.
3. Brahms's personal working copy of the first edition for piano solo (Rieter-Biedermann), in the possession of the Gesellschaft der Musikfreunde in Vienna.
4. The Rieter-Biedermann edition for two pianos.

REMARKS:

The concerto was published in 1861, but only in orchestral parts and for piano solo (source text 3). The score and the two-piano edition did not appear until 1875. A newly engraved score was published by C. F. Peters in 1918. The original title reads: "Concert für das Pianoforte mit Begleitung des Orchesters componiert von Johannes Brahms. Op. 15." Publication number 815.

The score, which, as has been mentioned, was published much later, contains a number of insignificant printing errors. The two editions for piano (source texts 3 and 4) were prepared with unusual care and are virtually free of error, so that in cases of discrepancies they were generally given the preference. These discrepancies follow:

In Movement 1, m. 78, the score gives Clarinet 1 a *c* on the fourth quarter; this has been corrected to *a*.

At the beginning of the piano solo in m. 91, the score lacks the indicated *p espress.* that appears in both piano editions. Similarly, the score lacks the "Poco più moderato" for the second theme of Movement 1 on both occurrences as well as the corresponding restoration of tempo "Tempo I."

In m. 255, the score gives the piano:

In m. 278, the score gives the piano upper staff as:

and, correspondingly, in mm. 281–282:

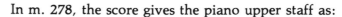

In his personal working copy, Brahms sketched the correction in pencil, and it is already adopted in source texts 3 and 4. In mm. 469–470 the score gives the piano:

A few striking departures from uniformity in details of instrumentation and phrasing in parts of the recapitulation that are otherwise exactly analogous to the exposition (especially noteworthy is the missing woodwind upbeat in m. 399 vis-à-vis the corresponding m. 175!) had to be retained since there is agreement in all source texts.

In Movement 3, m. 20, source text 3 gives the piano *d*-sharp in the upper staff; Brahms crossed out the sharp sign there, and this change was already made in source texts 1 and 4. At the last eighth note in m. 21, and likewise in m. 156, the score gives "poco sosten.," and two mm. later "a tempo." In the piano editions this nuance does not come until the last reappearance of the theme, in m. 309. In m. 232, the score gives the double bass *f* instead of *e*-flat. In m. 463 in the first piano edition the left hand has the octave *D* tied for eight mm. without new attacks. In the personal copy (source text 3) the ties are crossed out every other measure; this change was made in the score, but the ties remain in source text 4.

Numerous small errors in the score, especially missing accidentals, ties and slurs, staccato dots and the like in the piano part, were altered on the basis of source texts 3 and 4. The relative unreliability of the score in comparison to the piano editions is apparently due to the fact that, being published much later, it was not newly compared against the very carefully checked piano edition.

PIANO CONCERTO NO. 2 IN B-FLAT MAJOR, OP. 83

Source Texts:

1. The Simrock edition of the score.
2. Brahms's personal working copy of the score, in the possession of the Gesellschaft der Musikfreunde in Vienna.
3. The Simrock "Edition for Piano Solo."
4. The original MS, in the possession of Prof. Robert Freund in Budapest.

Remarks:

The concerto was published in 1882 by N. Simrock, Berlin, with the title: "Concert (No. 2 B dur) für Pianoforte mit Begleitung des Orchesters von Johannes Brahms. Op. 83." Over this is the dedication: "Seinem theuren Freunde und Lehrer Eduard Marxsen zugeeignet." Publication number 8263.

The score contains a few insignificant engraving errors. One of them is corrected in the personal copy (a missing flat sign in front of the *d* in the double bass, Movement 3, m. 44), which has no other handwritten entry. A mistaken natural sign in front of the *e*-flat in the Violin 1 part in Movement 3, m. 42 (Oboe 1 at the same point has *e*-flat, which also occurs in the piano solo edition) was eliminated. The solo edition includes no differences from the piano part in the score.

The original MS, which was obviously used as engraving copy, has numerous corrections in Brahms's hand, all of which involve details of instrumentation, as well as entries in another hand relative to details of the engraving process. A great number of small tempo changes added in blue pencil (Movement 1, m. 118 "animato," m. 128 "poco sostenuto," m. 286 "sostenuto," m. 291 "in tempo," m. 332 "un poco sostenuto," etc.) were crossed out again later — seemingly to avoid chopping up the tempo, but nevertheless a clear indication that the composer intended a certain freedom in performance. The original tempo indication of the finale was "Allegro non troppo e grazioso."

Vienna, Spring 1927　　　　　　　Hans Gál

EDITOR'S COMMENTARY

VIOLIN CONCERTO, OP. 77

SOURCE TEXTS:

1. Simrock's edition of the score, with the title: "Joseph Joachim zugeeignet. Concert für Violine mit Begleitung des Orchesters von Johannes Brahms. Op. 77. 1879." Publication number 8133.

2. Brahms's personal working copy of the printed score, in the possession of the Gesellschaft der Musikfreunde in Vienna. This contains a single correction involving not a printing error but an alteration. In Movement 1, in each of the mm. 336 and 337, the *c* in the Violin 1 and 2 parts is changed from a half note to a quarter note with staccato dot and quarter rest, thus corresponding to the violas, cellos and basses. The passage, which thus originally read:

was corrected here on this basis.

3. The original MS, in the possession of the firm of N. Simrock, Berlin. It contains, alongside many later pencil corrections in Brahms's hand, additional corrections in another hand in the solo violin part only, entries apparently made at the publisher's from a solo part that had been improved according to Joachim's suggestions. All these solo changes are purely technical ones aiming at a more idiomatic use of the instrument or a more brilliant effect. Thus, for example, in the finale, mm. 259 ff., the solo violin originally had:

Mm. 325 and 326 originally read:

Over this was entered as an improvement:

The definitive version uses the technical aspect of this alteration but reverts to the triplets. This final form was notated in the margin in Brahms's hand and crossed out later.

CONCERTO FOR VIOLIN AND CELLO, OP. 102

SOURCE TEXTS:

1. The score as published by N. Simrock with the full title: "Concert für Violine und Violoncell mit Orchester von Johannes Brahms. Op. 102." 1888, publication number 8964.

2. Brahms's personal working copy, with the correction of a single insignificant printing error, in the possession of the Gesellschaft der Musikfreunde in Vienna.

3. Brahms's original MS, in the possession of the Gesellschaft der Musikfreunde in Vienna, 76 quarto leaves. At the end the signature: "J. Brahms Thun in Sommer 87."

The printed score, apart from a few insignificant printing errors, is free of mistakes. In the last movement, m. 191, the second pair of horns has

in the MS as well as the printed edition; this is obviously an oversight and was corrected in the most suitable manner. The MS contains numerous pencil corrections added later, especially in the two solo parts. The MS differs from the printed score in many small details — corrections obviously done after the initial engraving, here again chiefly involving the solo instruments (largely, more effective versions of the figuration). Most likely, suggestions from the first two performers of the solo parts, Joachim and Hausmann, were taken into account here. The most interesting of these alterations follow:

Movement 1. In m. 5 the MS still lacks the indication "in modo d'un recitativo," etc.

In mm. 79–86 the sixteenth notes in the middle string voices were originally in three parts, with divided 2nd violins, thus:

etc. Similarly in the parallel passages mm. 197 ff. and 367 ff.

In m. 88, the next-to-last viola note, originally *e* (making parallel fifths with Violin 1!) was changed in the MS to *d.* The corresponding correction in the parallel passage, m. 374, was (obviously by oversight) omitted in the MS but included in the printed edition.

In m. 407, the solo violin, continuing the preceding figure, was originally given:

From the middle of the next bar on, the MS contains two different solutions written one above the other, neither of them in complete agreement with the printed version:

The upper system is in the hand of Joseph Joachim. Before the upbeat ("in tempo"), m. 415, the MS has a breathing pause (‖) drawn in a later time; it would be worthwhile considering the retention of this mark even though it was omitted again in the printed version.

Movement 2. From m. 73 on in the MS, the two soloists have:

Movement 3. From m. 149 to 156, the solo violin in the MS has only the upper voice of the printed version without double stops. A double-stop figure, but not yet the one in the printed score, is sketched in above mm. 149 and 150 in pencil:

In a completely similar way, from m. 180 on, the MS has a simpler figure for the solo violin with an alteration sketched in over it, but one that was again changed in the printed version:

In mm. 246 and 247 the solo violin lacks the triplet on the second eighth note; this is sketched in almost illegibly in pencil.

In m. 257 all source texts give the drum which is obviously an oversight, since before and after this spot the higher *e* is called for and Brahms always spells out a retuning carefully when he wants one.

Beginning with m. 304 in the MS, the solo cello figure is notated differently:

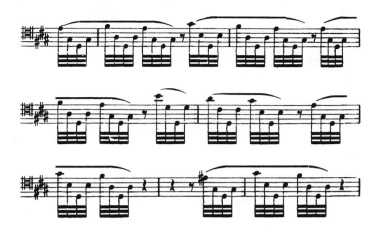

A mark "NB" in the margin points to the intended alteration.

From m. 330 on in the MS, the solo violin originally had only to repeat the triplet figure of the two preceding mm. two octaves above the cello. Over this were sketched (from m. 328) two different versions of the violin part and one of the cello part:

The uppermost of these three staves is in Brahms's hand, the two others in Joachim's.

VIENNA, SUMMER 1926   HANS GÁL

REVISIONSBERICHT

KLAVIER-KONZERT Nr. 1 DMOLL. Op. 15

VORLAGEN:

1. Die Partiturausgabe des Verlags Rieter-Biedermann (jetzt C. F. Peters in Leipzig).
2. Brahms' Handexemplar der Partitur, im Besitz der Gesellschaft der Musikfreunde in Wien.
3. Brahms' Handexemplar der ersten Klavierausgabe (Rieter-Biedermann), im Besitz der Gesellschaft der Musikfreunde in Wien.
4. Die Rieter-Biedermannsche Ausgabe für zwei Klaviere.

BEMERKUNGEN:

Das Konzert erschien 1861, jedoch bloß Orchesterstimmen und Klavierausgabe (Vorlage 3). Erst 1875 erschien die Partitur und die Ausgabe für zwei Klaviere. Eine neugestochene Partitur ist 1918 bei C. F. Peters erschienen. Der ursprüngliche Titel lautet: »Concert für das Pianoforte mit Begleitung des Orchesters componiert von Johannes Brahms. Op. 15.« Verlagsnummer 815.

Die, wie erwähnt, viel später erschienene Partitur enthält eine Anzahl unbedeutender Druckfehler. Den beiden Klavierausgaben (Vorlage 3 und 4), die ungemein sorgfältig bezeichnet und so gut wie fehlerlos sind, wurde deshalb, wo Differenzen bestehen, im allgemeinen der Vorzug gegeben. Solche sind nachstehend angeführt:

Im 1. Satz Takt 78 hat in der Partitur die 1. Klarinette auf dem 4. Viertel *c*, das nach *a* richtiggestellt wurde.

Beim Einsatz des Klaviersolos im 91. Takt fehlt in der Partitur die Bezeichnung *p espress.*, die in beiden Klavierausgaben enthalten ist. Ebenso fehlt in der Partitur beim Seitenthema des 1. Satzes beidemal das »*Poco più moderato*« und die entsprechende spätere Wiederherstellung »*Tempo I*«.

Takt 255 lautet in der Partitur das Klavier folgendermaßen:

Takt 278 lautet in der Partitur das obere System des Klaviers folgendermaßen:

und entsprechend Takt 281—282:

Im Handexemplar ist die Korrektur von Brahms mit Bleistift skizziert, die in den Vorlagen 3 und 4 bereits durchgeführt ist. Takt 469—470 lautet das Klavier in der Partitur folgendermaßen:

Einige auffallende Inkonsequenzen in Bezug auf Satz- und Phrasierungseinzelheiten in den der Exposition sonst genau konformen Teilen der Reprise (besonders auffallend der fehlende Holzbläserauftakt im Takt 399 gegenüber dem entsprechenden Takt 175!) mußten, da in allen Vorlagen übereinstimmend, bestehen bleiben.

Im 3. Satz Takt 20 steht in der Vorlage 3 im oberen System des Klaviers ♯ *dis*; das ♯ ist dort von Brahms gestrichen, was in den Vorlagen 1 und 4 bereits durchgeführt ist. Beim letzten Achtel im 21. Takt und ebenso im 156. Takt steht in der Partitur »*poco sosten.*«, zwei Takte später »*a tempo*«. In den Klavierausgaben steht diese Nüance erst bei der letzten Reprise des Themas, im 309. Takt. Im 232. Takt hat in der Partitur der Kontrabaß *f* anstatt *es*. Im 463. Takt hat in der ersten Klavierausgabe die linke Hand durch acht Takte die Oktave D gebunden, ohne Wiederanschlag. Im Handexemplar (Vorlage 3) sind die Bindebogen jeden zweiten Takt gestrichen, welche Änderung in der Partitur durchgeführt ist, wogegen in der Vorlage 4 noch die Bogen stehen.

Zahlreiche kleine Fehler in der Partitur, namentlich fehlende Versetzungszeichen, Bogen, Staccatopunkte u. dgl. im Klavierpart, wurden nach den Vorlagen 3 und 4 richtiggestellt. Die relative Unverläßlichkeit der Partitur im Vergleich zu den Klavierausgaben scheint dadurch erklärt, daß bei ihrem verspäteten Erscheinen offenbar keine neuerliche Vergleichung mit der sehr sorgfältig revidierten und bezeichneten Klavierausgabe vorgenommen wurde.

———————

KLAVIER-KONZERT Nr. 2 B DUR.   Op. 83

VORLAGEN:

1. Die Simrocksche Druckausgabe der Partitur.
2. Brahms' Handexemplar der Partitur, im Besitz der Gesellschaft der Musikfreunde in Wien.
3. Die Simrocksche »Ausgabe für Pianoforte solo«.
4. Die Originalhandschrift, im Besitz von Prof. Robert Freund in Budapest.

BEMERKUNGEN:

Das Konzert erschien im Jahre 1882 bei N. Simrock in Berlin, mit dem Titel: »Concert (No. 2 B dur) für Pianoforte mit Begleitung des Orchesters von Johannes Brahms. Op. 83«. Darüber die Wid-

Wien, im Frühjahr 1927.

mung; »Seinem theuren Freunde und Lehrer Eduard Marxsen zugeeignet.« Verlagsnummer 8263.

Die Partitur enthält wenige unbedeutende Stichfehler. Ein einziger ist im Handexemplar richtiggestellt (ein fehlendes ♭ vor *des* im Kontrabaß, 3. Satz, 44. Takt), das sonst keinerlei Eintragungen enthält. Ein falsches ♮ vor *es* in der 1. Violine im 3. Satz, 42. Takt (in der 1. Oboe steht gleichzeitig *es*, in der Klaviersoloausgabe ebenfalls *es*) wurde beseitigt. Die Soloausgabe zeigt keinerlei Abweichungen von der Klavierstimme der Partitur.

Die Originalhandschrift, die augenscheinlich als Stichvorlage benutzt wurde, zeigt zahlreiche Korrekturen von Brahms' Hand, die durchwegs Details der Instrumentation angehen, sowie stichtechnische Eintragungen von fremder Hand. Eine große Anzahl mit Blaustift hinzugesetzter kleiner Temporückungen (im 1. Satz Takt 118 »animato«, Takt 128 »poco sostenuto«, Takt 286 »sostenuto«, Takt 291 »in tempo«, Takt 332 »un poco sostenuto« u. a.) sind nachträglich wiederum gestrichen; anscheinend, um die Einheitlichkeit der Temponahme nicht zu gefährden, jedoch ein deutlicher Hinweis auf die Absicht einer gewissen Freiheit des Vortrags. Die Tempobezeichnung des Finales war ursprünglich »Allegro non troppo e grazioso«.

Hans Gál.

REVISIONSBERICHT

KONZERT FÜR VIOLINE, Op. 77

VORLAGEN:

1. Die Simrock sche Druckausgabe der Partitur, deren Titel lautet: »Joseph Joachim zugeeignet. Concert für Violine mit Begleitung des Orchesters von Johannes Brahms. Op. 77. 1879.« Verlagsnummer 8133.

2. Das Brahmssche Handexemplar der Druckausgabe, im Besitz der Gesellschaft der Musikfreunde in Wien. Dieses enthält eine einzige Korrektur, die aber keinen Druckfehler, sondern eine Änderung betrifft. Takt 336 und 337 im 1. Satz ist das c der 1. und 2. Violine aus einer Halben beide Male in eine Viertel mit Stakkatopunkt und folgender Viertelpause verwandelt, entsprechend den Bratschen und Bässen. Die Stelle, die also ursprünglich so lautete:

wurde demgemäß richtiggestellt.

3. Die Originalhandschrift, im Besitz des Verlags N. Simrock in Berlin. Sie enthält, neben vielen späteren Bleistiftkorrekturen von Brahms' Hand auch solche in fremder Schrift, und zwar bloß in der Solovioline, Eintragungen, die offenbar aus einer nach Joachims Vorschlägen verbesserten Solostimme beim Verlag gemacht wurden. Es handelt sich durchweg um rein technische Veränderungen in Hinsicht besserer Violinmäßigkeit oder brillanterer Wirkung. So lautete z. B. im Finale Takt 259 ff. in der Solovioline ursprünglich folgendermaßen:

Takt 325 und 326 lauteten ursprünglich:

Darüber ist, als Verbesserung, eingetragen:

Die endgültige Fassung geht, mit Benützung der technischen Seite dieser Änderung, wieder auf die Triole zurück. Diese letzte Form ist von Brahms' Hand, nachträglich durchgestrichen, an den Rand notiert.

KONZERT FÜR VIOLINE UND VIOLONCELL, Op. 102

VORLAGEN:

1. Die Partiturausgabe des Verlags N. Simrock, deren vollständiger Titel lautet: »Concert für Violine und Violoncell mit Orchester von Johannes Brahms. Op. 102.« 1888, Verlagsnummer 8964.

2. Brahms' Handexemplar, mit der Korrektur eines einzigen, unwesentlichen Druckfehlers, im Besitz der Gesellschaft der Musikfreunde in Wien.

3. Brahms' Originalhandschrift, im Besitz der Gesellschaft der Musikfreunde in Wien, 76 Blätter in Quartformat. Zum Schluß das Signum: »J. Brahms Thun im Sommer 87.«

Die Druckausgabe ist, von wenigen unbedeutenden Druckfehlern abgesehen, fehlerfrei. Im letzten Satz, Takt 191, steht im 2. Hörnerpaar ♮ sowohl in der Handschrift als in der Druckausgabe, was augenscheinlich ein Versehen ist und auf die nächstliegende Art richtiggestellt wurde. In der Handschrift stehen zahlreiche nachträgliche Bleistiftkorrekturen, namentlich in den beiden Solostimmen. In einer Menge kleiner Details weicht die Handschrift von der gedruckten Fassung ab, — Korrekturen, die augenscheinlich erst nach dem Stich vorgenommen wurden und vor allem wiederum die Soloinstrumente betreffen (größtenteils wirksamere Fassungen des Figurenwerks). Hierbei dürften wohl Ratschläge der beiden ersten Vertreter der Soloparte, Joachim und Hausmann, mitbestimmend gewesen sein. Die interessantesten dieser Änderungen sind nachstehend verzeichnet.

1. Satz. Im 5. Takt fehlt in der Handschrift noch die Anmerkung »in modo d'un recitativo« usw.

   Takt 79 bis 86 waren die Sechzehntel der Streicher-Mittelstimmen ursprünglich, mit geteilten 2. Violinen, 3 stimmig in folgender Weise geführt:

usw. Ebenso an den Parallelstellen Takt 197 ff. und 367 ff.

Takt 88 ist die vorletzte Note der Bratschen, ursprünglich *e* (Quintenparallele mit der 1. Violine!), in der Handschrift auf *d* korrigiert. Die entsprechende Korrektur an der Parallelstelle Takt 374 ist, offenbar aus Versehen, in der Handschrift unterblieben, in der Druckausgabe aber erfolgt.

Takt 407 war die Solovioline ursprünglich, in Fortsetzung der vorherigen Figur, folgendermaßen geführt:

Von der Mitte des folgenden Taktes an sind in der Handschrift zwei verschiedene Lösungen übereinander notiert, die beide mit der gedruckten Fassung nicht ganz übereinstimmen:

Das obere System ist von der Hand Joseph Joachims.

Vor dem Auftakt (in tempo) im 415. Takt ist in der Handschrift nachträglich in allen Stimmen eine Luftpause (‖) eingezeichnet, deren Einhaltung sehr zu erwägen wäre, obwohl sie in der gedruckten Fassung wieder weggeblieben ist.

2. Satz. Vom 73. Takt an lauten die beiden Soloinstrumente in der Handschrift folgendermaßen:

3. Satz. Vom 149. bis zum 156. Takt hat die Solovioline in der Handschrift bloß die Oberstimme der gedruckten Fassung, keine Doppelgriffe. Eine Doppelgriff-Figur, die aber mit der gedruckten auch noch nicht übereinstimmt, ist im 149. und 150. Takt mit Bleistift darüber skizziert:

In ganz ähnlicher Weise steht vom 180. Takt angefangen in der Handschrift eine einfachere Figur der Solovioline mit darüber skizzierter Änderung, die dann auch wieder in der gedruckten Fassung noch anders geworden ist:

Im 246. bis 247. Takt fehlt in der Solovioline die Triole auf dem zweiten Achtel, die mit Bleistift fast unleserlich dazu skizziert ist.

Im 257. Takt steht in allen Vorlagen in der Pauke *tr* , was augenscheinlich ein Versehen ist, da vorher und nachher das höhere *e* verlangt ist und Brahms eine Umstimmung immer ausdrücklich vorzuschreiben pflegt.

Vom 304. Takt angefangen ist die Figur des Solovioloncells in der Handschrift anders gelegt:

Ein »NB« am Rand deutet auf die beabsichtigte Änderung hin.

Vom 330. Takt an hatte die Solovioline im Manuskript ursprünglich bloß die Triolenfigur der beiden vorangegangenen Takte, in der Doppeloktave zum Solovioloncell, zu wiederholen. Darüber sind zwei verschiedene Fassungen der Violine und eine des Violoncells skizziert (von Takt 328):

Das oberste dieser drei Systeme ist von der Hand Brahms', die beiden andern sind von Joachim geschrieben.

Wien, im Sommer 1926.

Hans Gál.

Piano Concerto No. 1 in D Minor, Op. 15

16 PIANO CONCERTO NO. 1 IN D MINOR

PIANO CONCERTO NO. 1 IN D MINOR

PIANO CONCERTO No. 1 IN D MINOR

PIANO CONCERTO No. 1 IN D MINOR

PIANO CONCERTO No. 1 IN D MINOR

Piano Concerto No. 2 in B-flat Major, Op. 83

Allegro non troppo

Piano Concerto No. 2 in B-flat Major

PIANO CONCERTO NO. 2 IN B-FLAT MAJOR

Allegretto grazioso M.M. ♩ = 104

2 Flöten (Kleine Flöte)
2 Oboen
2 Klarinetten in B
2 Fagotte
4 Hörner in D / in B basso 1. 2. / 3. 4.

Klavier

1.Violine
2.Violine
Bratsche
Violoncell
Kontrabaß

Allegretto grazioso

Fl.
Ob.
Klar. (B)
Fag.

Klav.

1.Viol.
2.Viol.
Br.
Vcl
K.-B.

170 PIANO CONCERTO No. 2 IN B-FLAT MAJOR

Violin Concerto in D Major, Op. 77

202 VIOLIN CONCERTO IN D MAJOR

244 Violin Concerto in D Major

Double Concerto for Violin and Cello in A Minor, Op. 102

300 Double Concerto in A Minor